EVERYTHING SHARKS

NATIONAL GEOGRAPHIC

NATIONAL GEOGRAPHIC
KIDS™

EVERYTHING SHARKS

BY RUTH A. MUSGRAVE

NATIONAL GEOGRAPHIC

WASHINGTON, D.C.

CONTENTS

This eye-catching shark is found around the world near tropical islands and is known by many names, including tiburón de Galápagos, manô, Galapagoshaai, and Galápagos shark.

A blacktip reef shark gliding along the coast of Tuamotu Archipelago, French Polynesia

INTRODUCTION

STRUTTING THROUGH

THE OCEAN LIKE THE ULTIMATE ROCK STAR, sharks are elegant, dynamic, sophisticated predators with a dangerous reputation. Sharks are completely unaware of how they inspire and intimidate. (Or maybe they're just too cool to care!)

What makes sharks so awe inspiring? From nose to tail a shark's entire body is engineered for survival.

Unfortunately, there's an ugly side to fame and it's taking its toll on these superstars of the sea. To appreciate and save them, you really need to know EVERYTHING about sharks.

EXPLORERS' CORNER

**Hi! I'm Jennifer Hayes.
And I'm David Doubilet.**

Photographing and studying sharks has been our love and work for most of our lives. Sometimes it seems as if we're underwater more than above, but you'll understand why once you catch a glimpse of these magnificent animals. Look for this cartoon of David in the shark cage to indicate an Explorers' Corner where we'll share our experiences with sharks in the sea.

With teeth up to two inches (5 cm) tall, the white shark has the largest teeth of any living shark.

1
MEET THE SHARK

WHAT IS A SHARK?

FISH

SHARK

FISH

NOT A
SHARK

YOUR PET GOLDFISH MAY NOT

LOOK LIKE A (GREAT) WHITE, BUT IF YOU IGNORE THE big teeth and bad reputation (and squint a bit. . .) you'll see the resemblance. That's because sharks and goldfish are fish.

Fish live in the water, have gills (to breathe), and fins. Most fish, including sharks, have scales. There are about 32,000 kinds of fish found throughout the world. Even on its most ferocious day, though, no one could confuse a goldfish with a shark. A shark, and its close cousins rays and skates, are fish, but a different kind. How are sharks different from a typical fish?

THRILL OF THE GILL

A shark has five to seven gill slits (openings) on each side of its head. A bony fish has just one.

NOTHING IS PERMANENT

A shark's scales and teeth are not permanent. It loses and regrows them throughout its life.

BONELESS FISH

Unlike most fish, a shark's skeleton is made of cartilage (like your ear or nose bridge), not bone.

FIRM FINS

The rigid fins and tail of a shark do not bend, flutter, or fold up against the body like a bony fish.

BONELESS = AGELESS?

Scientists use bone, teeth, or scales to determine the age of a bony fish. Without bones or permanent teeth and scales, it is a challenge to determine the age and life span of sharks.

5 REASONS IT'S GOOD TO BE A SHARK

1 You're more famous than a rock star.

2 Your reputation is fierce.

3 You never have to brush your teeth or visit a dentist.

4 You have the most awesome and awe-inspiring dorsal fins in the sea.

5 You like school but never have homework.

SHARK BITE
RED TAIL SHARKS, POPULAR IN HOME AQUARIUMS, ARE BONY FISH, NOT SHARKS.

SUPER SHARK AWARDS

FASTER THAN A SPEEDING
BULLETFISH, LEAPING SMALL BOATS IN A SINGLE
bound. . .it's super shark. Most of the 450 to 500 shark species go about their lives in secrecy, but a few stand out. Here are some of the world's super sharks.

BEST BURP (AND BARK)

When threatened, a swell shark doubles its size by gulping water. Once safe it makes a dog-like bark and burps out all the water.

SHARK REVO-LUTION

Whirling like a top, a spinner shark snaps up schooling fish with such power it vaults out of the water, making two to four full spins midair.

FAN-TASTIC FISH

Whale sharks are the world's largest shark—and fish. Possibly reaching lengths up to 65 feet (20 m), it's larger than two city buses. Weighing up to 74,970 pounds (34,006 kg), it doesn't just tip the scales, it smashes them!

SHARK BITE   IT WOULD TAKE 117 DWARF LANTERNSHARKS (OR PENCILS) TO BE AS LONG AS A WHALE SHARK!

SPEED CHASER

Shredding the water at 31 miles per hour (50 kph), a shortfin mako shark is the world's fastest shark. Makos are faster than bottlenose dolphins (22 mph/35 kph) and killer whales (30 mph/48 kph). Their speed makes them too fast for most predators—except humans.

HIGH JUMP

A shortfin mako leaps 20 feet (6 m) above the water surface. That's higher than a giraffe's head. (No giraffes were hurt making this comparison.)

During the day, as many as 36 nurse sharks pile on top of each other as they rest in caves and crevices.

BEST DOG PILE

EXPLORERS' CORNER

The most dramatic thing in the ocean is a shark. White sharks appear and disappear like ghosts. A shark cage is the only safe way to observe and photograph larger, more aggressive sharks. It's especially unwise to get out if there is more than one shark!

One of the smallest sharks, the dwarf lanternshark is only 6.6 to 7.8 inches (17–20 cm)—about as long as a pencil.

PEEWEE PREDA-TORS

COOL SHARKS NEAR YOU

DIVE A METER OR A MILE,

AND YOU WILL FIND A

shark. Here are some exquisite examples of these elegant animals' ecosystems.

Usually found in water less than 13 feet (4 m) deep, the **LEOPARD SHARK** is common along the Pacific coast of North America from Oregon to Mexico.

Little is known about the dazzling **ZEBRA BULLHEAD SHARK** found along the coasts of Japan, China, Taiwan, Vietnam, and Australia.

The **TASSELLED WOBBEGONG** adds even more beauty to the coral reefs of New Guinea and Australia. It curls up in caves during the day and may eat any fish trying to share the space.

The **PRICKLY DOGFISH** gets its name from its super-rough scales. The best way to see this shark is from a deep-sea submersible off the coasts of New Zealand and Australia.

ASIA

PACIFIC OCEAN

AUSTRALIA

WORLDWIDE SHARKS

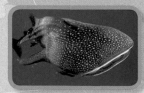

WHITE
Whether it's in the middle of the ocean or near the coast, white sharks (also called great whites) are found in nearly every ocean of the world.

LEMON
Lemon sharks hang out along the coast in waters as deep as 295 feet (90 m).

SCALLOPED HAMMERHEAD
Scalloped hammerhead sharks live close to shore throughout the world.

TIGER SHARK
Tiger sharks are found throughout the world in temperate and tropical seas.

WHALE SHARK
The giant of the sea, the whale shark lives in tropical and temperate waters worldwide.

ARCTIC OCEAN

EUROPE

NORTH
AMERICA

GREENLAND SHARKS chill in the North Atlantic and Arctic dining on seabirds, invertebrates, and dead whales. Indigenous people have used its hide for boots and teeth as knives.

One place to see groups of **SPINNER SHARKS** hunting schools of fish is in warm-temperate and tropical waters of the Mediterranean.

ATLANTIC
OCEAN

AFRICA

SOUTH
AMERICA

INDIAN
OCEAN

The **NURSE SHARK** is active at night in the mangroves, reefs, and rocky shores of the eastern and western Atlantic, the Gulf of Mexico, and eastern Pacific from Mexico to Peru.

The **BLACKTIP REEF SHARK** is a common shark in the reefs of the Mediterranean Sea, and Pacific and Indian Oceans.

This stunning beauty is a **PYJAMA SHARK** found along the southern tip of Africa. Don't let its looks fool you. It eats hagfish, bony fish, small sharks, and shark egg cases.

Map Key

 Polar waters

Temperate waters

Tropical and Subtropical waters

SHARK BITE SIX RARE SHARK SPECIES CALL THE FRESHWATER RIVERS OF BORNEO, AUSTRALIA, AND INDIA HOME.

ANTARCTICA

FROM SHORE TO OCEAN FLOOR

0 ft (0 m)

33 ft (10 m)

66 ft (20 m)

98 ft (30 m)

ft (40 m)

164 ft (50 m)

197 ft (60 m)

230 ft (70 m)

262 ft (80 m)

295 ft (90 m)

SHARK BITES
OFTEN HAPPEN WHEN
PEOPLE ACCIDENTALLY
TRIP OR STOMP
ON A SHARK AT THE BEACH.

Baby Pool

Bays, inlets, and shallow near-shore waters are important shark nurseries where pups can grow up away from larger predators. In one bay in the Gulf of Mexico, scientists found seven species of shark pups: blacktip reef, Atlantic sharpnose, bull, finetooth, bonnethead, scalloped hammer-head, and spinner.

Bonnethead Shark

Beach Buddies

Waders, surfers, and divers in Florida are usu-ally unaware that swimming nearby are sand devils, bonnet-head, blacktip, sandbar, spin-ner, scalloped hammerhead, and more.

Blacktip Reef Shark

Colorful Coral Sharks

Some might think sharks come in three colors: gray, light gray, and dark gray. But sharks that live in coral reefs dress for success with color and pattern.

Puffadder Shyshark

SHARK BITE THE GREAT LANTERNSHARK LIVES 14,764 FEET (4,500 M) DOWN—MORE THAN TWICE AS DEEP AS THE GRAND CANYON.

Wild Numbers

THERE'S ALWAYS

A SHARK NEARBY. Some sharks, like salmon, white, and whale, migrate long distances through different habitats. Others stay close to home.

49 megamouth sharks have been documented since first discovered in 1976.

95 percent of the oceans have yet to be explored.

12,000 feet (3,800 m) is the average ocean depth.

6,897 miles (11,100 km) in 99 days is how far and fast white sharks migrate from South Africa to Australia.

100 species of sharks are hunted for their fins, meat, oil, and body parts.

900,000 tons of sharks have been caught every year for the last 20 years. (Scientists suspect twice as many have actually been caught.)

Sharks of the Forest

Along the Pacific coast, exotic forests of giant seaweed called kelp (which can be 100 ft/30 m tall) provide a perfect home where sharks live, hide, and hunt.

Leopard Shark

Sharks in the Dark

Dive down 295 feet (90 m) and the sunlight is 10 percent as bright as it was at the surface. At 492 feet (150 m) you've lost 99 percent of the sunlight. Many sharks live even deeper where there is no sunlight at all. Even there, human activities such as fishing, pollution, and oil spills threaten their survival.

Megamouth Shark

A PHOTOGRAPHIC DIAGRAM

SHARK PARTS

Scales The scales are like tiny teeth, with a pulp cavity and enamel layer.

Liver The fat-filled liver provides buoyancy and stores energy. A basking shark's liver is 25 percent of its body weight.

Camouflage Sharks virtually disappear above and below. The darker back blends in to the dark sea below. The light-colored underside disappears in the lighter surface above. This camouflage is called countershading.

Skin Thick skin and scratchy scales make a shark's skin rough and tough. Some sharks, like carpet sharks, can change their skin color to blend into their surroundings.

Fins Fins help with stability and maneuverability, provide lift, and propel the shark through the water. The size and shape depends on the shark's lifestyle.

Gill Slits Sharks have five to seven gill slits. To respire (breathe), water goes through the mouth (or spiracles), over the gills, then out the gill slits.

Brain It's a myth that sharks are brain-less beauties. Hunting seals, sea lions, and dolphins takes strategy and planning.

Eye Some sharks have a nictitating membrane that covers and protects the eye.

Nostrils As much as two-thirds of a shark's brain is related to its sense of smell.

Tongue In most sharks, the small tongue has little known use. Mega-mouth and cookiecutter sharks have flexible tongues important for feeding.

Shape Cutting through the water is easier with this football-shaped body.

EXTRA PARTS

Barbels These projections feel and sense food.

Spiracles These openings bring water in and over the gills. It's a perfect adaptation for bottom-dwelling sharks so they can breathe (respire) without getting a mouthful of sand.

2

IT'S A SHARK'S LIFE

Most sharks are finicky eaters. But the tiger shark gobbles up fish, other sharks, seabirds, iguanas, sea snakes, sea turtles, and sea scraps such as garbage and carrion.

OH, BABY!

IF SHARKS COULD TALK,
"MAMA" AND "PAPA" WOULD NOT BE IN THEIR vocabulary. Sharks do not care for pups or guard eggs. Unlike bony fish, sharks do not have a larval stage. All pups come into the world a fully formed predator with a mouth full of teeth ready to hunt. Exactly how they come into the world varies. Some are born live, others hatch from an egg, and some do both!

A peek inside a dogfish shark's egg case shows the yolk sac attached to the pup.

IT'S NEVER A GOOD IDEA TO TICKLE A BABY SHARK UNDER ITS CHIN. SCIENTISTS **HAVE BEEN BITTEN** BY UNBORN SANDTIGER SHARKS WHILE EXAMINING THE MOTHER.

SOME SHARKS HATCH FROM AN EGG . . .
Many sharks hatch from a leathery egg. The developing pup gets all its nutrients from the yolk sac. Depending on the species and water temperature, some pups hatch in a month; others take more than a year.
Examples: Horn, bull, and swell sharks

Shark Pup

Yolk Sac

SHARK BITE WATER TEMPERATURE PLAYS AN IMPORTANT ROLE IN HOW QUICKLY THE EMBRYO HATCHES OR IS BORN.

YOU MUST BE YOLKING!

Sometimes one yolk isn't enough to grow on. In some species, when the embryo is the size of a paper clip, after it absorbs its own yolk, it eats the other eggs inside the female. Some species produce special eggs just for the embryos to eat. The sand tiger shark takes this up a notch. When the sand tiger embryo is about 4 inches (10 cm) long, it begins killing and eating the other embryos (inside the female). At birth, the surviving well-fed pup is 3 feet (1 m) long and is almost half the mother's size.

...SOME SHARKS ARE BORN LIVE...

Similar to a mammal, the developing pups get their nutrients from the mother. This style of birth allows the mother to successfully give birth to large litters.
Examples: blue and hammerhead

Newborn Numbers

2.4 inches (6 cm) long is the size of newborn dwarf lanternsharks and thorny lanternsharks.

25 inches (64 cm) is the length of a newborn whale shark.

300 eggs were found inside one female whale shark.

135 blue sharks were born in one litter.

24 months is the longest (documented) shark pregnancy.

...AND SOME ARE BORN THROUGH A COMBINATION OF BOTH!

A third group have an interesting combo of egg and live birth. Rather than releasing the egg into the ocean, the fertilized egg stays inside the female. The embryo gets its nutrients from the yolk sac, hatches and is completely developed before it is born live.
Examples: whale sharks and spiny dogfish

A lemon shark and newborn lemon shark pup

MAKING SENSE OF SHARK SENSES

IF THE CURRENT AND LIGHT ARE JUST RIGHT, A SHARK . . .

hears prey 820 feet (250 m) away.

smells blood one-half mile (1 km) away.

sees movement up to 50 feet (15 m) away.

feels the flutter of moving animals one to two body lengths away.

detects living animals from 20 inches (50 cm) away.

ONE WAY TO GET A SHARK'S

ATTENTION IS TO SWIM LIKE A WOUNDED ANIMAL. . . . or a person. Sounds of thrashing made by an injured animal attract sharks. People flounder and wallow like wounded prey rather than slip through the water like a healthy seal or fish. Sharks take notice of more than just sounds. They're attracted to smell, movement, and other signs of life. Check out sharks' mind-boggling senses.

LATERAL LINE A fluid filled canal, called the lateral line, runs down each side of a shark's body. The lateral line feels movement and vibration. The lateral line and sense of smell may work together to track ripples and scent made by moving fish.

SHARK BITE   WHITE AND OCEANIC WHITETIP SHARKS POKE THEIR HEADS OUT OF WATER TO PICK UP AIRBORNE SCENTS.

AMPULLAE Freckling the shark's snout are *ampullae of Lorenzini*. These are small sensory pits that detect electrical currents radiating from all (living) animals. This sense locates prey buried in sand, for example.

EYES In the light, our vision is about the same as a shark's. In the dark, however, a shark's eyes are ten times more sensitive to light. Reflective cells (called tapetum lucidum) in the back of the eye work like a mirror to reflect and double the available light.

NOSTRILS A shark's sense of smell is 10,000 times better than ours! Sharks use ocean currents to pick up scents from farther away. (Just as a breeze could lead you to a backyard BBQ.)

TASTE Do sharks savor the fish flavor? Scientists are unsure. Some sharks may use taste to decide if something is edible. Some sharks may use taste and smell together to find food. Maybe you can figure out how to run a shark taste test!

EXPLORERS' CORNER

Because sharks see contrasting colors well, we never wear a shark's favorite color, *yum yum yellow*. The lighter color shows up too well against the darker ocean water. When wearing dark wetsuits, we cover up our hands and legs so they don't look like flashes of fish. Sometimes sharks bite our strobe lights because they're attracted to the electrical pulse. They lose interest after tasting the hard plastic.

EATING IN STYLE

OCEAN EATS

Though a few sharks hunt large prey such as seals or whales, most hunt and eat much smaller prey. Below is a partial list of what various sharks throughout the world might eat.

1. sharks, sharks, and more sharks (some listed below)
2. abalones
3. anchovies
4. angel sharks
5. barracuda
6. basking sharks
7. billfish
8. bonitos
9. bluefish
10. blue sharks
11. butterfish
12. caribou
13. catsharks
14. chimaeras
15. cod
16. corals
17. cownose rays
18. crabs
19. croakers
20. cuttlefish
21. dogfish sharks
22. dolphins
23. eagle rays
24. eels
25. elephant fish
26. elephant seals
27. flatfish
28. flounder
29. fur seals
30. garbage
31. giant squid
32. gray whale calves
33. grunters
34. guitarfish
35. hakes
36. halibut
37. hammerheads
38. harbor seals
39. hermit crabs
40. herring
41. horseshoe crabs
42. houndsharks
43. jellyfish
44. krill
45. lancetfish
46. lanternfish
47. lanternsharks
48. lizardfish
49. lobsters
50. lumpfish
51. mackerels
52. mako sharks
53. marlins
54. mullet
55. needlefish
56. penguins
57. ocean sunfish
58. octopuses
59. oysters
60. parrotfish
61. pollocks
62. porcupinefish
63. porpoises
64. pufferfish
65. rays
66. remoras
67. rockfish
68. sailfish
69. salmon
70. sardines
71. scorpionfish
72. sculpins
73. sea anemone
74. seabirds
75. sea horses
76. sea lions
77. sea robins
78. sea snakes
79. sea squirts
80. sea turtles
81. sea urchins
82. seals
83. shrimp
84. skates
85. skipjacks
86. smelts
87. snails
88. snappers
89. squid
90. squirrelfish
91. soldierfish
92. sole
93. steelhead trout
94. surgeonfish
95. swordfish
96. striped bass
97. tuna
98. whale calves
99. whiting
100. worms (polychaetes)
101. wrasses

People are not on any shark's menu! Bites are usually accidental. Find out more on pages 38–39.

SO MANY SHARKS,

SO MUCH STYLE. HOW A SHARK HUNTS AND WHAT IT EATS DEPENDS ON THE SHAPE AND SIZE of its body and teeth. Schools of sardines, mackerels, anchovies, or herring become a swirling buffet for some sharks. Porbeagle, silky, and other sharks rocket through fish schools gobbling up dinner. Makos and blacktip reef sharks do a little dinner prep by herding fish into a tight ball.

SCANNERS

Like a living metal detector, a hammerhead shark skims along the ocean bottom, using its ampullae of Lorenzini to scan for prey hidden under the sand.

SHARK BITE A MAJOR PREDATOR OF MANY SHARKS IS ANOTHER SHARK.

STRAINING TO EAT

Whale, basking, and megamouth sharks filter fish and plankton from the ocean.

HIDE AND EAT

Wobbegongs blend into the ocean bottom, watching and waiting for prey to swim close enough to snatch.

SNEAK ATTACK!

Looking upward in search of the perfect silhouette, some sharks, including the white and tiger, lurk just deep enough to hide in the dark. When a fish, seal, or turtle swims overhead, the shark launches upward in a surprise attack.

OPEN WIDER?

As if a mouth full of razor-sharp teeth isn't enough, some sharks have a jaw-dropping ability. Really, their jaws drop! Unlike mammals, the shark's upper jaw is not fused to the skull. When biting, the upper and lower jaws drop and move forward, rotating the teeth outward. This gives the shark a larger bite or better suction to capture prey.

School Food

Sand tigers eat fish such as herring, snappers, remoras, eels, and bonitos.

SHARK BITE
SCIENTISTS CAN IDENTIFY THE SPECIES BY THE TOOTH AND BITE SHAPE.

BITES WITH PEARLY WHITES

A SHARK WOULD BANKRUPT THE TOOTH FAIRY.

THROUGHOUT ITS LIFE, A SHARK MIGHT LOSE 30,000 TEETH!

Sharks have rows and rows of teeth and not one is permanent. Pups even lose teeth before they're born. When a tooth falls out, one from the row behind replaces it. Depending on the species, a tooth may last a week or a few months. Sharks do not chew their food; they swallow it whole or in chunks. According to the food it eats, a shark's teeth are designed to slice, rip, tear, or crush food.

Fast Food

Makos snatch fast-swimming swordfish and tuna with spearlike teeth.

Cracked Crab

Horn sharks have two kinds of teeth. The front teeth hold prey, the back grind. They eat crabs, shrimp, sea urchins, sea stars, and small fish.

Supersize Meal

A white shark's teeth are serrated like a knife. It hunts large prey such as seals and sea lions.

Dine and Dash

The 19-inch-long (48 cm) cookiecutter hunts whales, tuna, marlin, and basking sharks. This quirky predator doesn't eat the entire prey, just a bite. Using its lips for suction and teeth for drilling, it bores out a chunk of flesh, leaving behind a small hole as seen in this dolphin below.

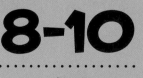

Tooth Totals

30,000 teeth are lost throughout a shark's life.

3,000 tiny teeth inside a whale shark's mouth

8-10 days to grow a new tooth

1/12 of an inch (3 mm) is the size of a whale shark's tooth.

A PHOTO GALLERY

SHARKS ALIVE!

SHARKS.
SO MANY SHAPES AND SIZES.
Here's a shout out to some of the many incredible sharks from around the world.

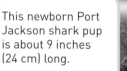

Silky sharks and yellowtail snappers dining together in the waters off the coast of Cuba

This newborn Port Jackson shark pup is about 9 inches (24 cm) long.

The mangroves of the Bimini Islands make a great nursery for these lemon shark pups.

Scientists captured this photo of a white shark breaching as it grabs a seal decoy in False Bay, South Africa.

Oceanic whitetip sharks are inquisitive, bold, and sometimes aggressive if divers aren't careful.

A whale shark's mouth is 4.6 feet (1.4 m) wide, almost as wide as a car.

This horn shark pup is in the middle of hatching from its spiral egg case.

The hammerhead shark's tough-as-nails reputation is false. They are wary and avoid people.

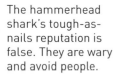

Luckily, this diver's close encounter with a white shark ended well. An adult white shark is more than three times longer than a person.

Adult sixgill sharks reach lengths up to 15 feet (4.8 m) and hunt whales and seals. Smaller sixgills hunt rays, sharks, and fish.

To find prey, a nurse shark uses its snout to root through the sand.

This swirling school of whitetip reef sharks searches for food.

3

SHARK SCHOOL

SHARK FAMILY TREE

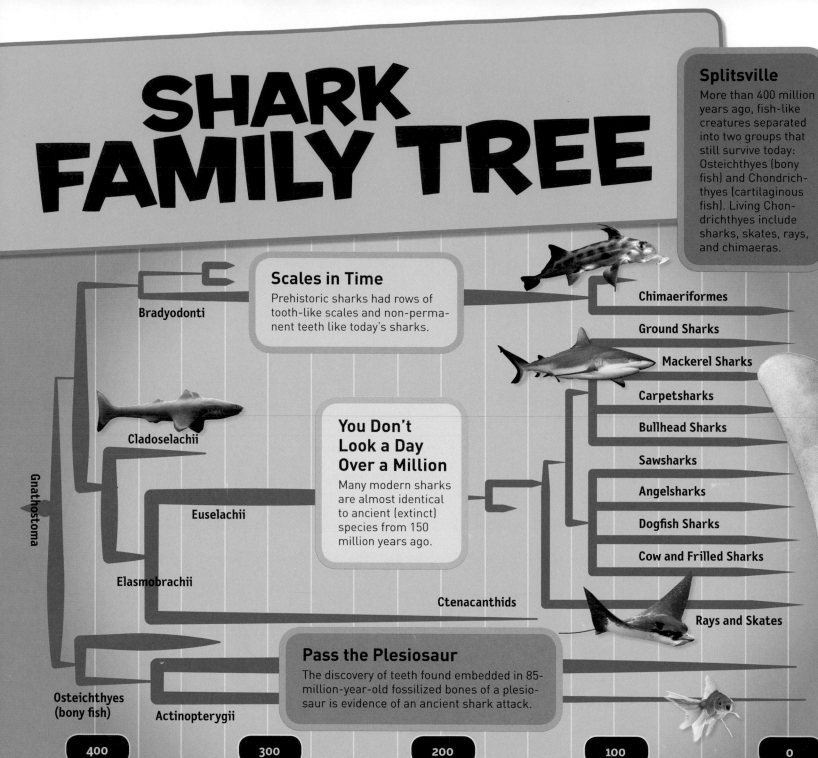

Splitsville
More than 400 million years ago, fish-like creatures separated into two groups that still survive today: Osteichthyes (bony fish) and Chondrichthyes (cartilaginous fish). Living Chondrichthyes include sharks, skates, rays, and chimaeras.

Bradyodonti

Scales in Time
Prehistoric sharks had rows of tooth-like scales and non-permanent teeth like today's sharks.

Cladoselachii

You Don't Look a Day Over a Million
Many modern sharks are almost identical to ancient (extinct) species from 150 million years ago.

Euselachii

Elasmobrachii

Gnathostoma

Ctenacanthids

Pass the Plesiosaur
The discovery of teeth found embedded in 85-million-year-old fossilized bones of a plesiosaur is evidence of an ancient shark attack.

Osteichthyes (bony fish)

Actinopterygii

Chimaeriformes
Ground Sharks
Mackerel Sharks
Carpetsharks
Bullhead Sharks
Sawsharks
Angelsharks
Dogfish Sharks
Cow and Frilled Sharks
Rays and Skates

400 · 300 · 200 · 100 · 0

MILLIONS OF YEARS AGO

Wow, You're Old!
The oldest known intact shark skeleton (a *Doliodus problematicus*) was recently found in Canada. This shark lived 409 million years ago.

BEFORE WHALES, BEFORE BIRDS,
BEFORE DINOSAURS—200 MILLION YEARS BEFORE DINOSAURS—

there were sharks. Sharks have rocked the seas for more than 400 million years. Tracing sharks throughout history is challenging because their cartilaginous skeleton is rarely preserved in fossils. Fortunately, fossilized teeth, scales, and spines give paleontologists a sketchy view of prehistoric sharks. The oldest known sharks have been identified from scales found in rocks almost 455 million years ago.

SHARKZILLA!

A white shark would be quaking in its fins at the sight of its ancient cousin *Carcharocles megalodon*. Based on fossil teeth, scientists estimate the largest were 60 feet (18.2 m) long and 55,125 pounds (25,000 kg). That's the size and weight of a fully loaded semitruck.

Old & New Numbers

600 species of rays and skates exist today.

1,100 species of Chondrichthyes (sharks, skates, rays, chimaeras) exist today.

3,000 fossil shark species have been identified.

450-500 species of sharks exist today.

SHARK BITE THE LARGEST TOOTH FOUND OF *CARCHAROCLES MEGALODON* MEASURES 7¼ INCHES (18.4 CM) LONG.

WEIRDEST SHARKS

SLEEK, ALOOF

SOPHISTICATED, ENERGETIC...
all part of a shark's DNA, right? As with all families, there are a few unattractive, quirky oddballs splashing around in the gene pool, too!

Goblin Sharks

In the deep dark sea, the flabby, pinkish goblin shark floats and waits. When dinner swims near, the shark snaps with a speed and reach enhanced by flexible jaws that shoot forward, distorting its ghoulish appearance even more.

Sawsharks

Before it's even born, a sawshark's teeth erupt. Luckily for the mother, the teeth lay flat against the rostrum (snout) until after it's born.

Greenland Sharks

The flesh of Greenland sharks is poisonous. This giant shark may snatch caribou right from the water's edge!

SHARK BITE STUDIES SHOW THAT A LEMON SHARK LEARNS 80 TIMES FASTER THAN A CAT!

Cookiecutter Sharks

Cookiecutter sharks add a twist to the camouflaging glow—an unlighted collar that lures prey. From below, the collar looks like a fish. When a would-be predator zooms in, the cookiecutter spins around and attacks first.

Lanternsharks

Ten percent of shark species are bioluminescent—they glow like a firefly. Light cells on the underside camouflage or hide the shark in the sunlight filtering down from above.

Frilled Sharks

Frilled sharks have changed very little since prehistoric times. These squid-eating, deep-sea sharks can grow as long as a Jeep. In 2009 scientists discovered a third frilled shark species.

OTHER ODDBALLS

Oceanic whitetip sharks hang out and hunt with pilot whales.

Shortfin makos are bright blue or purplish.

False eye spots on the backs of carpet sharks may trick predators.

Bull sharks occasionally swim 2,220 miles (3,573 km) up the Amazon River (up to Peru) and 1,800 miles (2,897 km) up the Mississippi River all the way to Illinois.

Angel Sharks

Hiding beneath the sand, the angel shark sits perfectly still and patiently waits and waits and waits for prey. Some wait weeks until the right meal swims along.

BUSTING SHARK ATTACK MYTHS

An example of a provoked bite due to a diver feeding a shark near San Clemente Island, California

PROVOKED vs. UNPROVOKED

Many shark "attacks" are provoked or caused by people touching, grabbing, feeding, or intentionally getting too close. Any wild animal can and will bite if frightened or threatened. A good rule of thumb: A shark is not a toy!

Because we share the shore with sharks, it sometimes leads to unprovoked attacks. Large sharks, such as white, tiger, and bull, hunt large prey in warm coastal waters. And people swim and play in shallow, warm coastal waters. Sharks do not hunt people, but sometimes our playtime overlaps with their mealtime.

ATTACK . . . SUCH A BIG WORD

FOR A LITTLE BOO BOO. Turns out, more than 90 percent of "attacks" in Florida are scratches and scrapes. To determine a more accurate level of injury, scientists and doctors have created a grading system (similar to what is used for burn victims): I (a scrape) to V (life threatening).

Scientists have identified three kinds of unprovoked attacks: hit-and-run, bump-and-bite, and sneak. Hit-and-run often happens where people swim and surf. Most likely, the shark has mistaken the person for prey in the churned up water. As soon as it bites, it realizes its error, takes off, and does not return. Injuries are usually small and below the knee.

Bump-and-bite and sneak attacks usually happen in deeper water. In a bump-and-bite attack, the shark circles and bumps the victim before biting. In a sneak attack, the shark attacks without warning. In both cases, the shark bites more than once and the injuries are severe, often leading to death.

Still worried? In the United States, you are 30 times more likely to be struck by lightning than be attacked by a shark.

> **MANY SHARKS STUFF THEMSELVES LIKE IT'S THANKSGIVING, THEN GO DAYS, EVEN WEEKS, BEFORE EATING AGAIN.**

To a hungry shark looking up, a person on a boogie board might look like a tasty seal.

ATTACK FACTS

Sharks are portrayed as killing machines. But we seem to be the deadliest creature in the sea!

0–5
... people might be killed by sharks a year.

70,000,000–100,000,000
... sharks are killed by people every year.

YOUR NUMBER MIGHT BE UP

...but probably not because of a shark. Yes, sharks sometimes kill people. It's very rare. How rare? Chances of a shark fatally attacking a person are 1 in 3,748,067. In 2009 in the United States, no one died from a shark attack. Still worried about being attacked? Relax, you are more likely to:

- win *American Idol*
- die in a sinkhole
- be struck by lightning
- die from the flu
- be killed by a deer
- hit a hole-in-one at golf
- drown (with no help from a shark)
- die in a bicycle accident
- be attacked by an alligator
- be injured fixing a toilet
- get bitten by a spider
- be killed by fireworks
- die from a cold
- be killed by a tornado
- stub your toe
- die from a fall
- become a professional football player

...and the list goes on and on! (NOTE: The list is not in statistical order.)

SHARK BITE BY BODY WEIGHT, A BONY FISH EATS TWICE AS MUCH AS A SHARK.

STUDYING SHARKS

At the Great Barrier Reef, Australia, researchers attach a satellite tag to the dorsal fin of a tiger shark.

IT'S CHALLENGING TRYING

TO STUDY ANIMALS THAT ROUTINELY TRAVEL hundreds, even thousands of miles or hide in the dark depths. Biologists use technology to virtually "hang" with sharks to reveal their secret world.

PLAYING TAG

Scientists followed Monty the mako shark 3,500-plus miles (5,633 km) and a salmon shark named Goldilox more than 5,400 miles (8,690 km) using electronic tags. Some tags track sharks in real time. The shark-GPS gives scientists up-to-the-minute data on a shark's location, distance, direction, and swimming speed. Other kinds of tags store data, such as location, depth, and water temperature, on a microchip. Scientists review the stored data after the chip falls off the shark.

A female oceanic whitetip shark takes a very close look at a scientist.

EXPLORERS' CORNER

A shark knows we're there before we have a clue about it. Once we were photographing dolphins in South Africa. A white shark that had probably watched us from the edge of visibility seemed to materialize out of nothing. Since we weren't in a cage we moved back to back to keep a 365-degree view of our guest. The curious shark made a wide circle and then vanished.

CRITTERCAM

One might think it'd be a wild ride hanging with tiger sharks, based on their reputation and diet. But Crittercam (a small camera temporarily attached to the shark) told a different story. Footage collected from tiger sharks showed them to be a bit boring, wandering through the sea in search of a trouble-free meal. No drama. No conflict. If the prey noticed the shark's approach, the tiger swam on, avoiding the extra work of fighting for its meal.

DNA

Analyzing DNA from whale sharks from the Indian Ocean, Pacific Ocean, and Caribbean Sea was like going to a family reunion. Turns out, though far apart, these populations were all closely related. That means whale sharks are interbreeding with others from distant parts of the world.

SHARK BITE   A SPINY DOGFISH CAN LIVE MORE THAN 100 YEARS.

BIG DOG OF THE SEA?

People quake at the sight of a white shark . . . but white sharks might feel the same about killer whales. After scientists observed a killer whale attack a white shark, all the white sharks in the area disappeared for several weeks.

Though some are larger, an adult male killer whale is about the same size as a large white shark—19 to 22 feet (5.8–6.7 m).

EATING

THE MOMENT A SHARK IS BORN, IT CAN SWIM AND HUNT.

Its instant skill to dart, sprint, and dive keeps it alive for the first hour, the first day. . . . Our lives are very different. Here are some examples.

SHARK COMPARISONS

YOU VS. A SHARK

FEARSOME FIN!

A large white shark's first dorsal fin is taller than 3.2 ft (1 m) tall. That's taller than a 4-year-old child!

If you ate like a shark, you'd only eat a small meal, like a piece of pizza, every few days. (And, you'd have to swallow it whole!)

PREGNANCY

A human mom is pregnant for about 40 weeks.
A gray reef shark is pregnant for 52 weeks.

NOSE

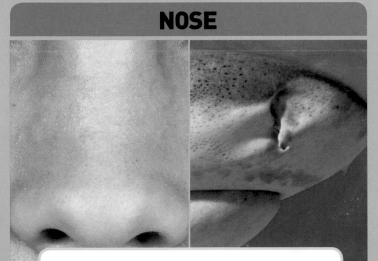

Before it is even born, a lemon shark can smell
10,000 times better than you can right now.

SKIN

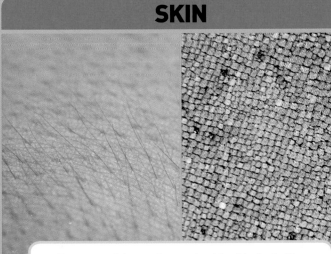

Because of the scales, a shark's skin feels like
sandpaper. Does yours?

PERMANENT TEETH

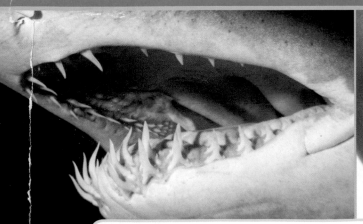

A shark starts losing teeth before it's even born, but it never has permanent teeth.
A six-year-old child starts replacing baby teeth with permanent teeth.

Don't let that silly grin fool you into getting too close. When pestered, a lemon shark will bite.

SWIM LIKE A SHARK

SOME SHARKS

RACE AT PHENOMENAL SPEEDS in pursuit of prey. Between hunts, they relax and cruise at much slower speeds of about 1.5 miles per hour (2.4 kph).

Ever wonder if you could outspeed a shark? Find out by measuring how far you swim (or run/walk) in five seconds. Compare your distance against the cruising and racing speeds of our sharks in a **Five Second Race**.

. . . a leopard shark would swim
9 FEET
(2.7 m). That's about three baseball bats end-to-end.

. . . a 14-foot-long (4.2 m) megamouth shark leisurely strolls
4.25 FEET
(1.3 m). That's like moving over two seats in a baseball stadium.

0 FEET	25 FEET	50 FEET	75 FEET	10
(0 M)	(8 M)	(15 M)	(23 M)	

... a shortfin mako zips
239 FEET
(73 m). On a soccer field, this speed demon could zoom from goal to goal. But the ball probably wouldn't survive!

GOLD MEDAL WINNER!

... a white shark can dash
183 FEET
(56 m). That's 1st to 3rd base! Heck, we know he'd make it all the way to home ... who'd be brave enough to tag him out?

... a blue shark easily swims
175 FEET
(53 m). It could sprint more than half a football field before the ref could throw the flag and say, "Shark on the field!"

... a quick 11-year-old can swim
20 FEET
(6.1 m). On a basketball court, that's the distance from the free throw line to the court line.

HOW TO AVOID BEING SHARK BAIT

Avoid wearing your herring hat, blood sausage necklace, and tuna-scented sunscreen...just kidding. To reduce the chances of accidentally meeting a shark experts suggest:

- Stay in groups and avoid swimming too far from shore.
- Avoid sunset or nighttime swims.
- Stay out of the water if sharks have been sighted.

- Avoid wearing bright colors (sharks see contrast very well) or shiny jewelry.
- Do not swim where sharks hunt (seal and sea lion rookeries, schools of fish, etc.).

- Do not touch, harass, grab, or feed sharks.
- Avoid entering the water if you are bleeding.
- Avoid places where others are fishing or dragging their catch with them.

SHARK BITE MOST SHARKS ARE COLD-BLOODED, BUT SOME ARE WARM-BLOODED.

| 125 FEET (38 M) | 150 FEET (46 M) | 175 FEET (53 M) | 200 FEET (61 M) | 225 FEET (69 M) | 250 FEET (76 M) |

SPOT THE SHARKS

CHECK OUT
THESE STEALTHY SHARKS
hiding in the rocks, sand, and coral. Their camouflaging colors match the ocean floor. Blotches, spots, and stripes also mimic the sunlight filtering through the water.

ABOVE: An ornate wobbegong from the South Pacific

NEAR RIGHT: Curled up in defensive position, this puffadder shyshark, sometimes called a Happy Eddie, isn't so happy.

FAR RIGHT: Hiding under the sand, the Pacific angel shark is ready to ambush its prey.

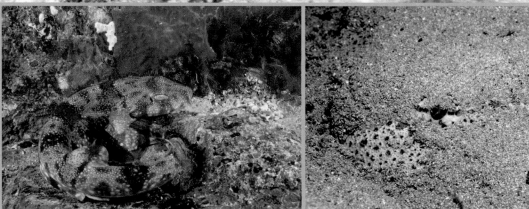

TOP: A swell shark blends into the rocky California coast.

BOTTOM: Carpet sharks, like this Indonesian speckled carpet shark, can change colors to blend in even better.

SPOT THE WHALE SHARK

Scientists use a whale shark's spots to identify individuals. It's a bit like finding constellations in the night sky.

SHARK BITE   COMPARING TOOTH SIZE TO BODY SIZE, COOKIECUTTER SHARKS HAVE THE LARGEST TEETH OF ANY SHARK.

SHARKS IN CULTURE

BEFORE THEY WERE

FEARED, SHARKS WERE REVERED.

Today, with 24-hour cable news, the Internet, instant messaging, and more, one shark bite becomes a global feeding frenzy of shark misinformation.

The irrational fear and hatred of sharks is new in human history. *Jaws* and other books, movies, and television shows vaulted sharks into the limelight, forever changing their image from rare and fascinating ocean predators to man-eating monsters pacing just offshore awaiting tourist season.

Throughout history, sharks held a place of honor, often given the role as protector or guardian. Sharks are represented in the art and tradition of the indigenous people of Hawaii, the Bidjogo people from Africa, the Aboriginal people of Australia, the Maori of New Zealand, and the Kuna people of the Panamanian islands. Swordfish, sharks, and rays were even found buried beneath an Aztec temple in Mexico City.

A shark carving from the Makira Province in the Solomon Islands

SHARK BITE THEY MAY HAVE AN ENORMOUS REPUTATION, BUT MOST SHARKS ARE ONLY THE SIZE OF A BASEBALL BAT!

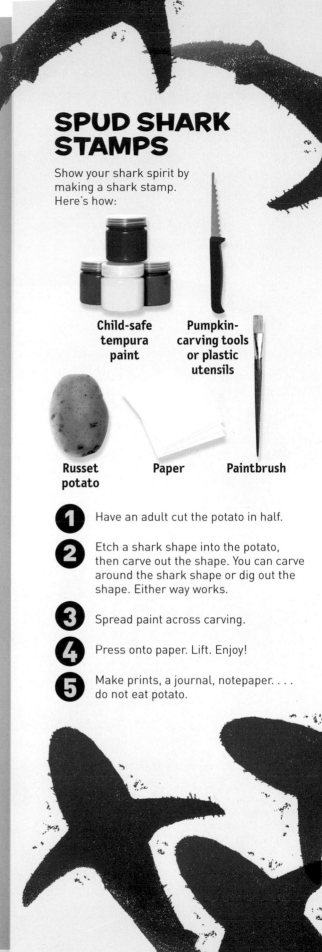

SPUD SHARK STAMPS

Show your shark spirit by making a shark stamp. Here's how:

Child-safe tempura paint

Pumpkin-carving tools or plastic utensils

Russet potato

Paper

Paintbrush

1 Have an adult cut the potato in half.

2 Etch a shark shape into the potato, then carve out the shape. You can carve around the shark shape or dig out the shape. Either way works.

3 Spread paint across carving.

4 Press onto paper. Lift. Enjoy!

5 Make prints, a journal, notepaper. . . . do not eat potato.

Popular movies such as *Finding Nemo* and *Jaws* portray sharks in different ways. LEFT: The shark is a mechanical model.

PLACES TO SAFELY SEE SHARKS

Oregon Coast Aquarium
Ocean World, Australia
Deep Sea World, Scotland
SeaWorld parks

Visit the American Association of Zoos and Aquariums website (*www.aza.org*) to find an aquarium near you.

FIN-TASTIC VIEW!

IF STANDING ON THE OCEAN FLOOR

WATCHING A SHARK GLIDE OVERHEAD SOUNDS APPEALING, THEN AN AQUARIUM IS FOR YOU. Aquariums raise appreciation and concern for animals. Plus, biologists learn about behavior, diet, food intake, and reproduction, knowledge that helps us better understand all sharks. Aquariums throughout the world are adding new dimensions so people can get closer to the sharks. Some have giant viewing areas, like the four-story-tall Giant Ocean Tank at the New England Aquarium. Others have acrylic tunnels where the sharks swim over and alongside you.

You can even put on a wetsuit and swim with whale sharks, hammerheads, zebra sharks, manta rays, and thousands of bony fish at the Georgia Aquarium. There, the sharks are carefully monitored, well fed (a.k.a. not hungry for you), and used to people in the water.

Tourists enjoy the breathtaking view of sharks at the Oregon Coast Aquarium.

FIN FUN

Whether it's an on-the-go hunter, a low-key drifter, or a bottom-dwelling shark, the fins tell you about a shark's lifestyle. Can you determine its swimming style by matching the tail to the shark?

Mako
FASTEST

Horn Shark
BOTTOM DWELLER

Catshark
SLOW

Blue Shark
FAST

Frilled Shark
SLUGGISH

Whitetip Reef Shark
WEAK SWIMMER

1

2

3

4

5

6

SHARK BITE THE SHARK TUNNEL AT DEEP SEA WORLD IN SCOTLAND IS 367 FEET (112 M) LONG. THAT'S LONGER THAN A FOOTBALL FIELD!

ANSWERS: Mako: 2; Horn Shark: 4; Catshark: 5; Blue Shark: 3; Frilled Shark: 6; Whitetip Reef Shark: 1

PHOTO FINISH

BEHIND THE SHOT WITH DOUBILET & HAYES

WORKING IN SHARK-
INFESTED WATERS ISN'T JUST AN
expression, it's a perfect day at work for photographers like David Doubilet and Jennifer Hayes.

Photographing sharks requires extensive planning and packing, traveling to remote areas, and spending weeks at sea and and hours underwater. Photographers must know the environment, the kinds of sharks in the area, whether they'll snorkel or scuba, and whether they need a boat or even a shark cage.

It's physical work to get close to the sharks, too. Photographers must swim, snorkel, scramble across rocky shores, or wade in sandy beaches while carrying cameras and other equipment.

After all that work and prep, sometimes the sharks never appear. But when everything works right, and the photographer is able to capture the majesty of a shark in a single photograph, it motivates, inspires, and encourages people to look at sharks in a new way.

Looking for sharks in new places and spaces, scientists come across a sleeping reef shark in an ocean cavern in the Gulf of Mexico. David Doubilet captured this magical moment.

AFTERWORD

CONSERVATION CONCERNS

Nets set for other fish often trap sharks.

SHARKS ARE AS IMPORTANT TO THE OCEAN AS THE WATER ITSELF.

THERE'S NO DOUBT THAT FOR THE LAST 400 MILLION YEARS, sharks and their relatives shaped ocean ecosystems. From meteors, volcanoes, ice ages, and continents moving and separating, sharks endured every catastrophic change. But they may not survive their most dangerous challenge—people.

Every hour, 11,415 sharks are killed for their fins, meat, skin, liver oil (squalene), cartilage, teeth, and sometimes accidentally. Products boasting the health and beauty benefits of shark oil and cartilage have flooded markets worldwide.

In Asia, eating shark-fin soup has become a popular sign of wealth. An estimated 73 million sharks, including hammerhead, blue, mako, basking, and dogfish, die for soup. The fins are cut off, then the shark is dumped into the sea to die.

The ocean feeds the world. Finding a balance between conservation and consumption is at the heart of sustainable fishing practices.

Worldwide, there is little or no regulation or protection. As shark hunting increases, populations decrease. The number of sharks has dropped by 90 percent in the Gulf of Mexico and 75 percent in the northwestern Atlantic. In the Mediterranean, more than 40 percent of sharks and rays are threatened with extinction.

Because sharks reproduce so slowly, even if shark fisheries stop today, scientists worry populations may not rebound.

BE A SHARK FRIEND!

FRUSTRATED BY WHAT'S HAPPENING to sharks? You are not alone; scientists are too. The lack of protection and support by governments and citizens is alarming. Most people still think sharks are villains, not victims. Millions of sharks need your protection, your voice. Years ago, people raised their voices to save the whales and it worked. It's now time to shout SAVE THE SHARKS!

To do that, WhaleTimes and the Shark Research Institute created *Fintastic Friday: Giving Sharks a Voice*. Join kids everywhere to promote shark conservation and protection efforts through "Sharks in the Park" rallies, signature gathering, and more. Raise your voice the second Friday in May—100 million sharks are counting on you.

The silky shark's name describes its skin texture. Overlapping scales are so tightly packed together the skin feels smooth.

AN INTERACTIVE GLOSSARY

A sicklefin lemon shark scatters a school of blue-striped snappers.

WANT TO SOUND LIKE A

SHARK EXPERT? These words will help. Check out the glossary word, test your shark smarts, then follow the page numbers to see the word in "action."

Adaptation
(PAGES 10-11, 16-17, 18-19, 24-25, 36-37)
A body part or behavior that helps an animal survive

Which adaptation leads to millions of shark deaths?
a. fins
b. teeth
c. scales
d. skin

Bioluminescence
(PAGE 37)
An adaptation that allows an animal to create or use light for camouflage, to find food, attract a mate, or as an alarm

What percentage of sharks are bioluminescent?
a. 50%
b. 1%
c. 10%
d. 25%

Camouflage
(PAGES 16-17, 18-19, 37, 48-49)
Color, pattern, and/or body shape that helps an animal hide or blend into its surroundings

Which of these sharks hides on the seafloor for weeks waiting for a meal?
a. porbeagle
b. salmon shark
c. whitetip reef shark
d. angel shark

Cartilage
(PAGES 10-11, 34-35, 56-57)
Flexible but sturdy tissue that shapes our ears, nose, and a shark's skeleton

Sharks' cartilaginous skeleton adds to the challenges of understanding them because . . .
a. cartilage is rarely found in fossils.
b. it limits the shark's size.
c. it's so flimsy, scientists can't touch sharks.
d. Both b and c.

Chondrichthyes
(PAGES 34-35)
The class of cartilaginous fishes that includes sharks, skates, rays, and chimaeras

What is the largest kind of Chondrichthyes?
a. white shark
b. manta ray
c. whale shark
d. basking shark

Embryo
(PAGES 22-23)
A baby animal developing inside an egg or female

In some species, if a shark embryo absorbs the entire yolk sac it...
a. does not survive.
b. is born early.
c. eats the other eggs inside the female.

Habitat
(PAGES 14-15, 16-17)
A plant's or animal's home

Which habitat is a shark's home?
a. sandy beach
b. coral reef
c. freshwater river
d. All of the above

Pup
(PAGES 16-17, 22-23)
A newborn or young shark

What do shark mothers feed their pups?
a. milk
b. nothing
c. chewed up fish
d. sardines

Predator and Prey
(PAGES 26-27)
A predator hunts and eats other animals. Prey is the animal that is eaten.

What is a favorite food of many sharks?
a. other sharks
b. seaweed
c. people
d. krill

Species
(PAGES 10-11, 12-13, 14-15, 16-17, 34-35, 36-37)
Scientists categorize or group plants and animals to help study and understand them. The categories start with a large general grouping, such as animals or plants (kingdom) down to the most specific or unique adaptations—species (kingdom, phylum, class, order, family, genus, species).

How many of the 32,000 species of fish are sharks?
a. 20,000
b. 40
c. 500
d. 1,000

Spiracle
(PAGES 18-19)
Openings on top of a shark's or ray's head that brings water over the gills

This adaptation is especially helpful to . . .
a. Whale sharks because it's hard to filter food and breathe.
b. Bottom-dwelling sharks and rays so they can breathe without getting a mouthful of sand.
c. None of the above

Squalene
(PAGES 18-19, 56)
A high-quality oil from a shark's liver

Compared to its body weight, how big is a basking shark's liver?
a. 15%
b. 25%
c. 50%
d. 3%

Tagging
(PAGES 40-41)
Attaching radio or satellite tags to an animal to track its movement

True or False: A satellite tag does *not* provide up-to-the-minute information on a shark's location.

a. True
b. False

ANSWERS: Adaptation: a; Bioluminescence: c; Camouflage: d; Cartilage: d; Chondrichthyes: c; Embryo: a; Habitat: d; Pup: b; Predator and Prey: a; Species: c; Spiracle: b; Squalene: c; Tagging: b

FIND OUT MORE

Love sharks and want to go deeper? Try these books and websites to learn everything else about sharks.

BOOK TITLES WITH A BITE

Sharks of the World
BY LEONARD COMPAGNO, MARC DANDO, AND SARAH FOWLER.
Princeton: Princeton University Press, 2005.

Face to Face with Sharks
BY DAVID DOUBILET AND JENNIFER HAYES.
Washington, DC: National Geographic, 2009.

WEBSITES

Florida Museum of Natural History
www.flmnh.ufl.edu

Great White Odyssey, National Geographic Channel
www.channel.nationalgeographic.com/episode/great-white-odyssey-3628

International Shark Attack Files
www.flmnh.ufl.edu/fish/sharks/isaf/isafabout.htm

Shark Bay Ecosystem Research Project
www.fiu.edu/~heithaus/SBERP

Shark Research Institute
www.sharks.org

Shark School, San Diego Natural History Museum
www.sdnhm.org/kids/sharks

To REM, I miss you every day. RM

Acknowledgments
Thank you to all the dedicated researchers working to save the sharks. A special thanks to Jeremy Vaudo, Florida International University; Dr. Tom Deméré, San Diego Natural History Museum; and Dr. Tamara Frank, Harbor Branch Oceanographic Institute/Florida Atlantic University. Your insight and knowledge were invaluable.

Published by the National Geographic Society
John M. Fahey, Jr., *President and Chief Executive Officer*
Gilbert M. Grosvenor, *Chairman of the Board*
Tim T. Kelly, President, *Global Media Group*
John Q. Griffin, *Executive Vice President;*
   President, Publishing
Nina D. Hoffman, *Executive Vice President;*
   President, Book Publishing Group
Melina Gerosa Bellows, *Chief Creative Officer,*
   Kids and Family, Global Media

Prepared by the Book Division
Nancy Laties Feresten, *Vice President,*
   Editor in Chief, Children's Books
Jonathan Halling, *Design Director, Children's Publishing*
Jennifer Emmett, *Executive Editor, Children's Books*
Carl Mehler, *Director of Maps*
R. Gary Colbert, *Production Director*
Jennifer A. Thornton, *Managing Editor*

Staff for This Book
Jennifer Emmett, Priyanka Lamichhane, *Project Editors*
Eva Absher-Schantz, *Art Director*
Lori Epstein, Annette Kiesow, *Illustrations Editors*
Erin Mayes, Chad Tomlinson, *Designers*
Kate Olesin, *Editorial Assistant*
Grace Hill, *Associate Managing Editor*
Lewis R. Bassford, *Production Manager*
Susan Borke, *Legal and Business Affairs*
Madeleine Franklin, *Editorial Intern*
Janice Gilman, *Illustrations Intern*

Manufacturing and Quality Management
Christopher A. Liedel, *Chief Financial Officer*
Phillip L. Schlosser, *Senior Vice President*
Chris Brown, *Technical Director*
Nicole Elliott, *Manager*
Rachel Faulise, *Manager*
Robert L. Barr, *Manager*

Captions
Front Cover: A great white shark shows his razor-sharp teeth as he thrashes out of the water.
Page 1: Caribbean reef sharks glide over a coral reef in the Bahamas.
Pages 2-3: Beautiful blue sharks silhouetted in the California sun

 The National Geographic Society is one of the world's largest nonprofit scientific and educational organizations. Founded in 1888 to "increase and diffuse geographic knowledge," the Society works to inspire people to care about the planet. National Geographic reflects the world through its magazines, television programs, films, music and radio, books, DVDs, maps, exhibitions, live events, school publishing programs, interactive media and merchandise. *National Geographic* magazine, the Society's official journal, published in English and 32 local-language editions, is read by more than 35 million people each month. The National Geographic Channel reaches 310 million households in 34 languages in 165 countries. National Geographic Digital Media receives more than 13 million visitors a month. National Geographic has funded more than 9,200 scientific research, conservation and exploration projects and supports an education program promoting geography literacy. For more information, visit nationalgeographic.com.

For more information, please call 1-800-NGS LINE (647-5463) or write to the following address:
National Geographic Society
1145 17th Street N.W.
Washington, D.C. 20036-4688 U.S.A.

Visit us online at www.nationalgeographic.com/books

For librarians and teachers: www.ngchildrensbooks.org

More for kids from National Geographic: kids.nationalgeographic.com

For information about special discounts for bulk purchases, please contact National Geographic Books Special Sales: ngspecsales@ngs.org

For rights or permissions inquiries, please contact National Geographic Books Subsidiary Rights: ngbookrights@ngs.org

Paperback ISBN: 978-1-4263-0769-0
Library binding ISBN: 978-1-4263-0802-4

Printed in United States of America
11/WOR/2